# PARENT AN ENDOR: THIS BOOK!!

C000132093

"Just like Volume 1, though this book – Volume 2 – was also written for children, it is an excellent stress reliever for adults as well! After all, laughter *is* the best medicine. I plan to use some of these jokes on my friends."

~Rowena Arrieta, World-class International Classical Pianist, Finalist and Laureate at the VII Tchaikovsky International Music Competition, Mother of two. http://bit.ly/RowenaArrietaPianist

I'm a grandfather of several grandkids and many kids to whom I've become like a grandfather. It's great to have a Joke and Riddles book that is not only FUN, but also clean! I highly recommend this book loaded with good, clean riddles, jokes and brain teasers. It's a wholesome book, which is somewhat of a rarity these days.

~Matt Buchanan, Operations Manager, Father of 4, Grandfather of 10, and Great Grandfather of 2.

As a grandmother, I enjoy reading clean, fun books to my grandchildren. This book fits the bill!! It's loaded with chapters of riddles, jokes, and brain teasers! I highly recommend **Volume 2** of "The Amazing Book of Riddles, Jokes, Knock-knock Jokes and Brain Teasers." And get **Volume 1** as well.

I plan to give these FUN books away to my grandchildren and the many children in my life -- for their birthdays, or for Christmas.

~Leslie Bower – Grandmother to 11, Real Estate Investor, and #1 Bestselling Author


Here is another great family-friendly joke and riddle book by Team Morey! As a grandmother it's important for my grandbabes to read wholesome yet fun books and this latest joke book by James, Jackie Michael, and Alyssa certainly fits the bill. If you haven't gotten their first book **"The Amazing Book of Riddles, Jokes, Knock-knock Jokes and Brain Teasers: Loads of FUN, Smiles and Laughter for Kids, Friends, Parents, Grandparents and Relatives (Riddles and Jokes Book 1)"** I highly recommend it. My kiddos loved Volume 1 and they *will love Volume 2 as well.*

~Sharon Best, Mother of two, Grandmother of four [so far], Life Coach


*As a grandmother, I'm always on the lookout for clean, fun books to read or to give to my grandchildren and other children in my life. This book is excellent! It's full of laugh-out-loud riddles, jokes, and brain teasers! Get this book for children in your family, your neighborhood, your school, and your church community. It'll be a BIG hit!*

~Dr. Becky Slabaugh #1 International Bestselling Author, Keynote Speaker, Licensed Clinical Pastoral Counselor, Mother of 2 Sons and Grammie to Tatum and Maisy Grace. www.InnerTreasuresMinistries.com

# YOUR FREE GIFT FOR CHECKING OUT OUR BOOK

Thank you for checking out our book! Our family would like to give **you** a FREE gift!!

Jim and Jackie's business friend – Jay Boyer – who's a Children's Book Bestselling Author and who makes thousands of dollars every month from his children's books, did a value-packed webinar called "**How to Write and Publish a #1 Bestselling Children's Book**."

Click here now to watch it ➔
https://bit.ly/ChildrensBookJackieMorey1

If you've always wanted to write a Children's Book, **this** is the webinar to watch. You'll even discover one of the *best niches* to write children's books for! Click the link below to access your FREE gift now...

➔ https://bit.ly/ChildrensBookJackieMorey1

# The Fantastic Book of Jokes, Riddles, Brain Teasers, and Knock-knock Jokes

MORE Loads of FUN, Smiles and Laughter for Kids, Friends, Parents, Grandparents and Relatives

Jackie Morey, James R. Morey, Michael Morey and Alyssa Morey

**Published by**
Customer Strategy Academy, LLC
16212 Bothell Everett Hwy, Suite F111, Mill Creek, WA 98012

Author Jackie Morey's email:
CustomerStrategyAcademy@gmail.com
As of this publication, Michael and Alyssa are still minors – so if you wish to connect with them, please do so only via their Mom's email address above. Thank you. ☺

**Limits of Liability and Disclaimer of Warranty**

**Disclaimer**

**Copyright Use and Public Information**

Paperback ISBN: **978-1-7332501-8-4**

## James's Dedication

To my wonderful, talented, amazing, beautiful and captivating Bride – Jackie, and our talented, fun-loving, energetic children – Michael and Alyssa. I enjoyed the many hours of laughing, "rolling on the floor", and occasionally groaning while developing this book. [The "groaner-jokes" are not included in this book. ☺ ]

## Jackie's Dedication

To my extraordinary Husband Jim – who is incredibly witty, topnotch at puns, and enjoys making me laugh right before bedtime, causing me to roll on the floor laughing!

To our two intelligent, creative and wise children – Michael and Alyssa – who both thoroughly enjoy jokes, riddles, knock-knock jokes and brain teasers! Indeed, having a cheerful heart is good for everyone (Proverbs 17:22), and I've enjoyed creating and sharing these jokes, riddles and brain teasers with you.

To my dear friends Sharon, Gloria, Evelyn, Kelly, Cheri, Laurie, to my siblings, all my nephews and nieces, to our extended families and friends in the U.S., Canada, and all over the world who love to laugh. I hope you enjoy this book! We invite you to invest in at least 10 more to give away to the many kids in your lives who love to laugh and enjoy good, clean fun!

## Michael's Dedication

To my sister Alyssa, to Mom and Dad, to Ninong Tong, Ninang Jen, Josh and Caleb, Ninong Ugee, Kuya Jiggs, Tito Tatan, Kuya Raphael, Uncle Mike, Aunt Becky, Uncle Carlos and Calo, to all my relatives in the U.S. and Canada, to all my teachers, and all my friends – especially Roman, Landen, Dalen, Noah, Levi, Ben, Micah, JJ, and the Reynolds Family.

And to all the kids and grownups in the world who want to laugh out loud with their friends and family.

## Alyssa's Dedication

To Mom and Dad, to my brother Michael, to Ninong Tong and Ninang Jen, Josh and Caleb, Ninang Joyce, Ate Danielle, Tita Ana Lou, Mr. and Mrs. Best, Grandpa Matt and Grandma Gigi, Auntie

Ev, Aunt Pam and Ivana, all my friends – especially Hannah, Allinore, Royee, Isla, Elise, Grace, Ruby, Mary, Megan, Olivia, the Samodien Family, Alyssa B., and Vrinda.

To all the kids, parents, grandparents and other grownups all over the world who want to have good, clean FUN with their friends and family – we have a lot of these clean jokes, riddles, and brain teasers for you in this book.

# TABLE OF CONTENTS

# FOREWORD

*"He will fill your mouth with laughter; your lips will spill over into cries of delight."* ~ Job 8:21 The Voice

**Volume 1** of "The Amazing Book of Riddles, Jokes, Knock-knock Jokes and Brain Teasers" brought smiles and laughter to our grandchildren and family.

9-time #1 International Best Selling Author Jackie Morey and her son Michael are back with **Volume 2** and *lots more* to laugh about!

And this time they've **co-written Volume 2** with Jackie's husband multiple #1 International Bestselling Author James Morey, and their daughter Alyssa.

My husband and I giggled our way through this book – **Volume 2** of "The Amazing Book of Riddles, Jokes, Knock-knock Jokes and Brain Teasers." The Star War Riddles were brilliant...and there's a BONUS Word Search puzzle for you as well!

If you want to have knee-slapping fun you need to read this book!

**_Dr. Becky Slabaugh, Ph.D._**
Licensed Clinical Pastoral Counselor
Life Coach, Guest Radio Co-Host and Ordained Minister
Multiple #1 Best Selling Author
www.InnerTreasuresMinistries.com

# CHAPTER 1

## Soup-to-Nuts
## [Food Riddles]

Q: Where do hamburgers go dancing?
A: At a meat-ball.

Q: How do pickles celebrate their birthdays?
A: They relish the moment.

Q: What does the salad say to the tortilla?
A: Lettuce taco 'bout it (Let us talk about it.)

Q: What do you call a fake noodle?
A: An IMPASTA (impostor)

Q: What did the carrot say to the farmer?
A: I'm rooting for you!

Q: What do you have to add to soup to make it gold soup?
A: Fourteen carrots (carats)

Q: Why did the pickle go to the doctor?
A: He was feeling dill. (play on words: ill)

Q: Why did the tomato blush?
A: Because it saw the salad dressing.

Q: Why are candy-swirls so easy to play tricks on?
A: Because they're suckers.

Q: What do you call a can opener that doesn't work anymore?
A: A can't opener

Q: When a lemon is sick, what do you do?
A: Give it lemon-Aid.

Q: What kind of fruit do twins love the most?
A: Pears (pairs)

Q: Why did the melon jump into the lake?
A: It wanted to be a watermelon.

Q: What's a duck's favorite taco topping?
A: Quackamole!

Q: How do ducks make pancakes?
A: They use Bis-quack!

Q: What do you call a crate of ducks?
A: A box of quackers!

Q: What is a duck's favorite type of popcorn?
A: Quacker Jacks!

Q: What is the radius of a pumpkin?
A. Pi.

# CHAPTER 2

# Weather and Water Riddles

Q: What did the cloud say to the wind?

A: You blow me away!

Q: How did the rain tie its shoes?

A: In a rainbow

Q: How did the lightning leave the party?

A: In a flash

Q: What are sleeping twisters?

A: Torna-doze

Q: What did the beach say when the tide came in?

A: Long time no sea!

Q: What's something that falls but will never hit the ground?

A: The temperature.

Q: What does a rain cloud wear under his raincoat?

A: Thunderwear!

Q: Why does it snow in the winter?

A: Because snow would melt in the summer.

# CHAPTER 3

## Knock-knock Jokes

Knock-knock

Who's there?
Ben
Ben who?
Ben knocking for ages, please let me in.

Knock-knock

Who's there?
Pickle
Pickle who?
Pickle little flower to give to your Mom.

Knock-knock

Who's there?
Spell
Spell who?
Ok, W-H-O!

Knock-knock

Who's there?
Brent
Brent who?
He's Brent out of shape!

Knock-knock

Who's there?
Scold
Scold who?
Scold outside, let me in!

Knock-knock

Who's there?
Cargo
Cargo who?
Car go, "Beep, beep! Vroom, vroom!"

Knock-knock

Who's there?
Annie
Annie who?
Annie body want to go on a picnic?

Knock-knock

Who's there?
Toodle
Toodle who?
Toodle-loo to you, too!

Knock-knock

Who's there?

11

Hurry
Hurry who?
Hurry-cane coming, let me in!

Knock-knock

Who's there?
Harry
Harry who?
Harry come! Ready or not! (Hide-and-Seek)

Knock-knock

Who's there?
Everglade
Everglade who?
Boy, am I everglade to see you!!

Knock-knock

Who's there?
Nana
Nana who?
Nana your business!

Knock-knock

Who's there?
Ben
Ben who?
Ben knocking for 10 minutes, where were you?

Knock-knock

Who's there?
Cereal
Cereal who?
Cereal pleasure to meet you! (It's a real pleasure to meet you!)

Knock-knock

Who's there?
Barry
Barry who?
Barry nice too meet you. May I come in now?

Knock-knock

Who's there?

Your Mom

Your Mom who?

Your Mom! Now open the door or you're grounded. ☺

Knock-knock

Who's there?

Police

Police who?

Police let us in. It's raining outside!

Knock-knock

Who's there?

Shelby

Shelby who?

Shelby comin' round the mountain when she comes!

# CHAPTER 4

# Tree Riddles and Plant Jokes

Q: What does a tree yell at a sporting event?
A: I'm rooting for you!!

Q: What is a tree's least favorite month of the year?
A: Sep-timber.

Q: How many peaches grow on a tree?
A: All of them!

Q: What's the saddest seed?
A: A weeping willow

Q: What did one tree say to his neighbor tree after the lumberjack left.
A: You're stumped!

Q: What is a tree's favorite game?
A: Follow the Cedar (play on words: Leader)

Q: What does a tree drink?
A. Root beer!

Q: What did the big flower say to the little flower?
A: Hi, bud!

Q: What did recently-lumberjacked Tree B say to Tree A when the latter asked the former a very difficult question?
A: I'm stumped!

Q: Why shouldn't you tell secrets in a cornfield?
A: There are too many ears.

Q: What has thousands of ears but can't hear at all?
A: A cornfield.

Q: What kind of tree fits in your hand?
A: A palm tree.

Q: Why did the seed shiver?
A: Because it lost its coat.

Q: What do you call a sad strawberry?
A: A blueberry.

# CHAPTER 5

# Star Wars Riddles

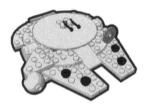

Q: What do you call a bird of prey that lives a thousand years?
A: A millennium falcon!

Q: What do you call a relay competition between The Millenium Falcon, an X-Wing Fighters and Tie Fighters?
A: A space race
[Note: This riddle will make its appearance in

another chapter ☺ Get ready! See if you can remember the answer!]

Q: How did Obi-Wan Kenobi store his jam?
A: He used Jar-Jar Binks

Q: What do you call someone who tries hard to be a Jedi?
A: Obi-Wannabe

Q: What candy did the Jedi invent?
A: Light-savers! (Lifesavers)

Q: What did Yoda's master say when young Yoda first started his Jedi training?
A: He's green!

Q: How did Yoda do, in his battle against Emperor Palpatine?
A: He came up short!

Q: Why can't you count on Yoda to pick up the tab?
A: Because he's always a little short.

Q: Why are Jedis so good at fractions?
A: Because they know how to use the fourth! (Force)

Q: Where did Darth Vader get his pet rodent?
A: The planet Mouse-tafar (Mustafar)

Q: How did Darth Vader know what Luke Skywalker got him for his birthday?
A: He felt his presents.

Q: Which bounty hunter is good at playing the guitar?
A: Boba Fret (Boba Fett)

Q: How did Yoda try to convince Obi-Wan Kenobi from getting married?
A: Yoda said: "Go be Wan Kenobi" (One Kenobi)

Q: What were Obi-Wan Kenobi and his wife called?
A: We-Be-Two Kenobi

Q: Which program do Jedi use to open PDF files?
A: Adobe Wan Kenobi.

Q: Which Jedi had a musical career?
A: Bon Jovi-Wan Kenobi.

Q: What do you call a pirate droid?
A: Arrrrr-2 D2.

Q: What droid always takes the long way around?
A: R2-Detour.

Q: What is Yoda's favorite car manufacturer?
A: To-Yoda (Toyota)

Q: What do you call a plastic Yoda?
A: Toy-yoda (Toyota)

Q: Why did Darth Vader turn off one light?
A: Because he prefers it on the dark side.

Q: How does Darth Vader like his toast?
A: On the dark side.

Q: What do you call Chewbacca when he gets chocolate on his fur?
A: A chocolate chip Wookie!

Q: How is bubble gum similar to a Wookie?
A. It's Chewy!

Q: What do you call a bounty hunter from the south?
A: Bubba Fett!

Q: Which Star Wars character works at a restaurant?
A: Darth Waiter!

Q: What happens when Jedi dogs turn bad?
A: They join the Bark Side.

Q: How do Ewoks communicate?
A: On their Ewokie-talkies!

Q: Why did episodes 4, 5, and 6 come before 1, 2, and 3?
A: In charge of planning, Yoda was.

Q: What's the most popular Star Wars movie in Italy?
A: The Phantom Venice.

Q: Where do Sith go shopping?
A: At the Darth Maul! (mall)

Q: Why did Darth Vader go to the music store?
A: To find the hidden rebel bass.

Q: Which Jedi was also an Italian pastry chef?
A: Obi-Wan Cannoli.

Q: What's a baseball player's least favorite Star Wars movie
A: The Umpire Strikes Back.

Q: What do sand people use to locate their enemies?
A Tuscan radar.

Q: What do sand people call their librarians?
A: Tuscan readers.

Q: What did Obi-Wan say to Luke at the rodeo?
A: "Use the horse, Luke!"

Q: What did the dentist say to Luke Skywalker?
A: May the floss be with you!

# CHAPTER 6

## Alphabet Riddles

Q: What letter of the alphabet can you use to call someone's attention?
A: A (Hey!)

Q: What letter of the alphabet is a bird?
A: J (Jay or Bluejay)

Q: What letter of the alphabet do pirates like to say a lot?
A: R (Arrrr!)

Q: What letter of the alphabet is wet
A: C (sea)

Q: What letter of the alphabet is a beverage
A: T (tea)

Q: What letter of the alphabet stings?
A: B (bee)

Q: What two letters of the alphabet sneeze a lot?
A: H-U (achoo!)

Q: What letter of the alphabet means "Yes" or something's "Fine"?
A: K (Okay)

Q: What letter of the alphabet is always surprised?
A: O (Oh!)

Q: What letter of the alphabet is in VeggieTales?
A: P (Pea)

Q: What letter of the alphabet is cross-eyed?
A: W (Double U)

Q: What letter of the alphabet is always philosophical?
A: Y (Why)

Q: What letter of the alphabet is always waiting in line?
A: Q (queue)

Q: What letter of the alphabet do I love most?
A: U (You)

Q: What letter of the alphabet must you protect from dust, sand and particles?
A: I (Eye)

Q: What letter of the alphabet has a leak?
A: S (Essssss)

Q: What letter of the alphabet is used as a conjunction?
A: N (And)

Q: What letter of the alphabet means "former"?
A: X (Ex, as in ex-teacher)

Q: What letter of the alphabet screams on a rollercoaster?
A: E (Eeeeeeee!)

Q: What letter of the alphabet is a name?
A: L (Elle)

Q: What letter of the alphabet is a possibility?
A: F (If)

Q: What letter of the alphabet is a nickname?
A: D (Dee)

Q: What other letter of the alphabet is also a nickname?
A: M (Emm as a nickname for Emma)

Q: What letter of the alphabet is "we" in German?
A: V (Germans pronounce the English word "we" as "vee")

# CHAPTER 7

# Animal Riddles and Brain Teasers

Q: Where do cows go for entertainment?
A: The mooooooooovies.

Q: What do you call a cow that plays the saxophone?
A: A moo-sician.

Q: What do cows read?
A: They read CATTLE-logs.

Q: Why was the cow afraid?
A: He was a cow-herd (coward).

Q: What do you call a cow spying on another cow?
A: A steak out (stakeout).

Q: Where do milkshakes come from?
A: Nervous cows!

Q: What's a cow's favorite drink?
A. LeMOOnade.

Q: What do cows like to put on their sandwiches?
A. MOOstard!

Q: What brand of car do cows like to drive?
A: MOO-stangs (Mustangs)

Q: Where can you find out more about cows'
paintings and art?
A: At the MOO-seum.

Q: How do you keep a bull from charging?
A: Take away its credit card!

Q: What do you call a bull who sleeps all the time?
A: A bull-dozer!

Q: Why are cats good at video games?
A: Because they all have nine lives

Q: What kind of sports cars do cats drive?
A: Fur-arris

Q: What kind of sports cars do sheep drive?
A: Lamb-borghinis

Q: What kind of sports cars do cows drive?
A: Moo-seratis

Q: What kind of key opens a banana?
A: A mon-key!

Q: What is a librarian's favorite pre-historic creature?
A: A pterodactyl. Because the p is always silent.

Q: What animal wears the biggest shoes?
A: The one with the biggest feet!

Q: What did the Papa Octopus say to his son before a dangerous trip?
A: Stick with me, I'll take care of you.

Q: What's the difference between a violin and a fish?
A: You can tune a violin, but you can't tuna fish!

Q: How do you communicate with a fish?
A. Drop it a line.

Q: What's a snake's strongest subject in school?
A: Hiss-tory.

Q: What do bumblebees chew?
A: Bumble gum.

Q: Where does a polar bear keep his money?
A: In a snow bank

Q: What's a chicken's favorite sign when there's a fire?
A: Egg-zit (Exit)

Q: What are chickens' favorite word when they agree with you?

A: Egg-zactly (Exactly)

Q: Why are fish very smart?
A: Because they live in schools.

Q: What's the most expensive fish called?
A: A goldfish.

Q: Why did the pony get sent to his room?
A: Because he wouldn't stop horsing around!

Q: Why couldn't the pony sing at the concert?
A: Because she was just a little hoarse! (horse)

Q: What do you call a Bear with no ears?
A: A "B"!

Q: Which animal at the zoo eats with its tail?
A: All of them. They can't take their tails off.

Q: What did the fisherman say to the magician?
A: Pick a cod, any cod!

Q: What two flowers can be found at the zoo?
A: Tiger lily and Dande-lion

Q: On which day do lions prefer to eat people?
A: Chews-day!

Q: Why wouldn't the shrimp share his vast wealth?
A: Because he was a little shellfish!

Q: How do prawns and clams communicate?
A: With shell-phones!

Q: What animal goes well with toast?
A: A jelly fish

Q: What do you call a fish with a tie and tuxedo?
A: soFISHticated

Q: What sea animal is very strong?
A: A mussel (play on words: muscle)

Q: What kind of photos will you find on a turtle's phone?
A: Shell-fies (selfies)

Q: What do you call a turtle that is famous?
A: A shell-ebrity.

Q: What is the most famous type of animal in the sea?
A: A starfish.

Q: How can the fish market charge such cheap prices?
A: They use economy of scale.

Q: What do you call a fish with two knees?
A: A two-knee fish!

Q: Why do they build *fish* ladders in dams?
A: So that the fish don't have to *scale* the walls

Q: What language do fish speak?
A: Finnish

Q: Where do fish sleep?
A: On a water bed.

Q: What are beavers' favorite salad dressing?
A. Branch dressing.

Q: Where does Spider-Man do research when he needs to find out something?
A: The World Wide Web.

Q: Which country has more fish than anywhere else in the world?
A: Finland

Q: What's a sleeping dinosaur called?
A: A dino-snore.

Q: What do you call a blind dinosaur?
A: Doyouthinkhesaurus? (Do you think he saw us?)

Q: What kind of explosions do dinosaurs like?
A. DINOmite!

Q. What do you get when you cross a pig with a dinosaur?
A. Jurassic Pork.

Q: What do you call it when a dinosaur crashes his car?
A. A Tyrannosaurus WRECK! (play on words: Tyrannosaurus Rex)

Q: If a seagull flies over a sea, what flies over the bay?
A: A bagel (play on words: bay-gull)

Q: What's the most popular name for a baby boy fish?
A: Gil (play on words: gill)

Q: What bird can write?
A. PENguin!

Q: Where does a penguin go to visit his aunt?
A. AUNT-arctica!

Q: What does an eagle use to write with?
A. A bald point pen!

Q: What did one sheep say to the other?
A: After ewe!

Q: Where do sheep go on their vacations?
A: To the Baaaaaa-hamas!

Q: What do you call an elegant dancing sheep?
A: A baaaa-lerina.

Q: How do you make an octopus laugh?
A: With ten-tickles! (tentacles)

Q: What question do owls like to ask a lot?
A: Who? Who?

Q: What question does the philosophical owl ask?
A: Why? Why?

Q: What does the schedule-conscious owl ask?
A: When? When?

Q: What did the buffalo say when his little boy went to school?
A: Bison! (Bye, son!)

Q: What do you call a bear with no teeth?
A: A gummy bear.

Q: Why don't ants ever get sick?
A: Because they have anty bodies.

Q: What did the frog order at McDonald's
A: French flies and Diet Croak

Q: What do you call an alligator in a vest?
A: An investigator

Q: Why can't a leopard hide?
A: Because he's always spotted.

Q: What kind of bird works at a construction site?
A: A crane.

Q: What is a duck's favorite part of the news?
A: The feather forecast.

Q: What is a duck's favorite ballet?
A: The Nutquacker!

Q: What is a duck's favorite animal at the zoo?
A: Quackodiles. (crocodiles)

Q: What kind of movies do ducks like to watch?
A: Duck-umentaries.

Q: What time do ducks get up?
A: The quack of dawn.

Q: What do ducks use to fix things around their house?
A: Duck tape!

Q: What kind of duck is a criminal?
A: A robber ducky!

Q: What was the goal of the detective duck?
A: To quack the case, of course.

Q: What do you call a 100-year-old ant?
A. An ANT-ique

Q: What kind of event do spiders love to attend?
A: Webbings (play on words: Wedding)

Q: What does a spider wear to her wedding?
A: A webbing dress. (Play on words: wedding dress)

Q: What does a bear say when he gets confused?
A: I bear-ly (barely) understand.

Q: What kind of snake would you find on a car?
A: A windshield viper!

Q: Why are snakes difficult to fool?
A: You can't pull their leg.

Q: Why can't you trust zookeepers?
A: They love cheetahs (cheaters).

Q: What kind of jungle cat is no fun to play games with?
A: A cheetah!

Q: How do elephants talk to each other long distance?
A: On the elephone!

Q: What's a shark's favorite bible story?
A: Noah's Shark.

Q: What's a shark's favorite science fiction TV show?
A: Shark Trek.

Q: How did the hammerhead do on the Math exam?
A: He nailed it.

Q: What did the Dalmatian say after she had a huge meal?
A: That hit the spot.

Q: Why did the dalmatian go to the eye doctor?

A. Because he kept seeing spots.

Q: Did you hear what happened to the flea circus?

A: The dog act stole the show!

Q: What type of dog is great at telling time?

A: A watch-dog.

Q: Why did the puppy get really good grades in class?

A: He was the teacher's pet.

Q: What type of pizza do dogs like to order?

A: Pup-eroni pizza.

Q: What did the dog say when he sat on sandpaper?

A: Ruff!

Q: What do you get when you cross a dog and a calculator?

A: A friend you can count on.

Q: What do dogs say to each other before eating?

A: Bone appetit! (Bon appetit)

Q: Why are dogs like phones?
A: Because they have collar IDs

Q: Why are spiders great software developers?
A: They like finding bugs.

Q: Can a kangaroo jump higher than the Seattle Space Needle?
A: Of course! The Seattle Space Needle can't jump!

Q: Where do horses live?
A: In neighhh-borhoods.

Q: What do you call a horse that lives next door?
A: A neighhh-bor!

Q: Where do horses go when they are very ill?
A: To the horse-pital!

Q: Why did the horse sail on a ship?
A: He was in the Neighhh-vy!

Q: What do monkeys wear when cooking?
A: Ape-rons!

Q: What kind of monkey flies through the air?
A: A hot air baboon!

Q: What's a kitty cat's favorite color?
A: Purrrr-ple.

Q: What is a cat's favorite car?
A Catillac!

Q: What is the unluckiest type of cat?
A: A catastrophe!

Q: What do cats eat on hot days?
A: Mice cream.

Q: There are ten cats on a boat. One jumped off, how many are left?
A. None, because they were all copy cats!

Q: What do you get when you cross a crocodile and a rooster:
A: A croc-o-doodle-doo

Q: Which kind of tree grows chicken?
A: A poul-tree! (poultry)

Q: What day do chickens fear the most?
A: Fry-days.

Q: What kind of jobs do funny chickens have?
A: They are comedi-hens!

Q: What do pigs use when they are ill?
A: Oinkment.

Q: Why is getting up in the morning like a pig's tail?
A. It's twirly. (play on words: Too early)

Q: What do you call a pig that does karate?
A pork chop.

Q: Why should you never share a bed with a pig?
A: They hog the blankets!

# The Three Ways of
# Escape Brain Teaser

You are trapped in a room and there are 3 doors. Each door has something behind it.

The first door has two hungry lions that have not eaten in four years.

The second door has electric lasers all across the room.

The third has three ninjas ready to attack.

Q: Which door would you pick to go through?

A. The first door because the lions would be dead if they hadn't eaten for 4 years!

# CHAPTER 8

# All About Sports

Q: What do you call a soccer player who loves arithmetic?
A: A Mathlete!

Q: Why is Cinderella terrible at soccer?
A: Because she keeps running away from the ball!

Q: Why do bowling pins have such a hard life?
A: They're always getting knocked down.

Q: What did the football coach say to the broken vending machine?
A: I want my quarter back!

Q: Why didn't the dog want to play football?
A: It was a boxer!

Q: What would a feline use to play baseball
A: A cat bat
[Note: This joke will make its appearance in another chapter. ☺ Get ready! See you if you'll remember the answer.]

Q: What animal can you always find at a baseball game?
A: A bat!

Q: How is a baseball team similar to a pancake?
A: They both need a good batter!

Q: Which superhero is a pro at hitting home runs?
A: Batman.

Q: What has 18 legs and catches flies?
A: A baseball team!

Q: What runs around a baseball field but never moves?
A: The fence!

Q: What's a sheep's favorite game?
A: Baaa – dminton!

Q: Why did the golfer wear two pairs of pants?
A: Just in case he got a hole in one!

Q: Why do basketball players love donuts?
A: Because they can dunk them!

Q: What kinds of stories do basketball players tell?
A: Tall tales!

# CHAPTER 9

## Tongue Twisters

Silly subtraction surprises Shelby.
Silly subtraction surprises Shelby.
Silly subtraction surprises Shelby.
Silly subtraction surprises Shelby.
Silly subtraction surprises Shelby.

Ron ran past tents in the past tense.
Ron ran past tents in the past tense.
Ron ran past tents in the past tense.
Ron ran past tents in the past tense.
Ron ran past tents in the past tense.

If you must crossly cross a coarse cross cow across a crowded cow crossing, cross the coarse cross cow across the crowded cow crossing carefully.
If you must crossly cross a coarse cross cow across a crowded cow crossing, cross the coarse cross cow across the crowded cow crossing carefully.

Legolas loves leftover lego Eggos.
Legolas loves leftover lego Eggos.
Legolas loves leftover lego Eggos.
Legolas loves leftover lego Eggos.
Legolas loves leftover lego Eggos.

Scramble bramble tumble angle
Scramble bramble tumble angle
Scramble bramble tumble angle
Scramble bramble tumble angle
Scramble bramble tumble angle

A tutor who tooted the flute tried to tutor two tooters to toot. Said the two to the tutor, "Is it harder to toot or to tutor two tooters to toot?"
A tutor who tooted the flute tried to tutor two tooters to toot. Said the two to the tutor, "Is it harder to toot or to tutor two tooters to toot?"

Pad kid poured curd pulled cod.
Pad kid poured curd pulled cod.
Pad kid poured curd pulled cod.
Pad kid poured curd pulled cod.

# CHAPTER 10

## The Three-Legged Pig

Once upon a time, there was a salesman named John who sold farm equipment. Salesman John visited Farmer Bob one day to see if he needed any supplies for his tractor or parts.

While John was saying hello, a 3-legged pig came up to him.

After discussing the parts that Farmer Bob needed for the tractor, John asked him, "So, what's up with the 3-legged pig?"

Farmer Bob proudly exclaimed, "Oh, that pig. That pig is some pig! That pig is a hero!"

John asked, "Why?"

Farmer Bob replied, "Well, a few weeks ago, the barn caught fire. I was inside dozing in the hay. I would've been a goner if it weren't for that pig! He rushed into the flames, grabbed me and pulled me out to safety!"

Then John asked, "So is *that* where he lost his leg?"

Farmer Bob replied, "Oh no, no. He was a little singed but he was fine, just fine."

Then John asked, "So how *did* he lose his leg?"

Farmer Bob said, "Well, a week after that, I was out in the field working on my tractor, and forgetfully, I left the motor running. I thought it was in neutral, my shoulder hit the lever and put it into gear. So I was caught there by my pant leg. Those sharp seeder blades were heading towards me. I thought for sure I was going to be cut to shreds! I was in the midst of saying my last prayer, when the pig came up, grabbed me by his teeth and pulled me to safety *again*! That's twice he saved my life in that many weeks!"

So John asked, "So *that's* how he lost his leg?"

Farmer Bob said, "Oh, no, no! We were both fine."

And so John asked, "Come on, Farmer Bob! How *did* he lose his leg?"

Then Farmer Bob said, "Just not two days ago, a big tornado came up...you heard about it. I was dozing on the sofa. If that tornado hit the house I would've been a goner for sure! But the pig ran in and woke me up. The whole family and I headed down to the shelter. But as the pig was coming down, the door slammed on his leg, there it was, exposed for the twister."

And so John said, "Ohhhh...so *that's* how he lost his leg!"

Farmer Bob replied, "Oh, *no*, *no*. The twister missed the house, we're all fine, the pig was good."

By now, exasperated, John exclaimed, "So *how* did the pig lose his leg?!"

To which Farmer Bob replied, "Well, a special pig like that, you don't eat him all at once!"

Then Farmer Bob added, "So, John, you want to come in and have a slice of ham?" ☺

[We'd like to give credit where credit is due.
This joke is courtesy of our relative Mike L.
Disclaimer: No animals were harmed
in the writing or retelling of this joke.]

# CHAPTER 11

# PUN FUN!!

## Oh, what "PUN" it is to ride our car to the music store!

One afternoon, I (Jackie) walked into a music store with my two children, to ask about leasing a saxophone and a violin for them.

The manager treated me and my children *very poorly* – he even yelled at us!

Well, I guess you could say that this caused some heart***strings*** of dis-***chord*** (discord).

But instead of getting bitter and resentful, here's what we did: Our family was given lemons, and we turned them into lemonade!!

After I told my Husband all about the incident, he and I had an interesting *pun* conversation.

Here's how it went...

**Husband**: Oh-h-h-h my, I'm sad that this happened to you, my Love! He was very *sharp* with you, wasn't he? That conversation sure didn't strike *a chord* with you! Are you sure you don't you want to go back and settle the *score*?

**Me**: Well, he'll reap what he sows. Besides, I've just written a review and given the store a poor 1-star rating. Their sales will likely go *flat* if he carries on the same way with other customers.

**Husband**: Well, I hope the Company Owner will take *note* of that manager's terrible behavior.

**Me**: You're right. That music company needs to do a much better job at training their *staff* in Customer service.

**Husband**: Yes, exactly, Honey. In this case, the right training will be *key* to their success.

**Me**: Indeed. And if they don't train them in manners and customer service, they'll lose more sales if they don't change their *tune*.

**Husband**: Exactly. And that won't make any company owner's heart *sing*.

**Me**: Well, I do forgive him from my heart. I guess we can now put all this to *rest*.

**Husband**: Yes, that's *music* to my ears. Besides, we don't want to *string* it along too far, would we?

The End

# CHAPTER 12

# Rhyming Riddles

One morning, I (Jackie) woke up with the thought: Rhyming Riddles!!

Hmmm...I had never heard the phrase "rhyming riddles" before. Suddenly, a flood of rhymes entered my mind such as: cat-mat

Wow! This could be one of the chapters for our riddles and joke book!!

Without further ado, this is the Rhyming Riddles chapter.

Q: What do you call a math expert who totally bombs on a math competition?
A: A Math Hero Zero

Q: What's another name for a snowstorm magician?
A: Blizzard Wizard

Q: What do you call a corner for bookworms?
A: A book nook

Q: What do you call a corner made for a castle chess piece?
A: A rook nook

Q: What do you call a kitty's rug?
A: A cat mat

Q: What do you call an overweight feline or kitty?
A: A fat cat

Q: What's another name for a chicken coop or enclosure?
A: A hen pen

Q: What do chickens write with?
A: A hen pen

Q: What do you call a conversation combined with a stroll
A: A talk walk

Q: What's another name for a lamb's honk
A: A sheep beep

Q: What do you call a Canus Majoris (heavenly body-oriented) automobile?
A: Star Car

Q: What do you call a fortress that NBA players could build?
A: A ball wall

Q: What do you call a chime signal located at the place where people draw water from underground?
A: A well bell

Q: What do you call a reptile magician?
A: A lizard wizard

Q: What's a cute name for a barber's customer's seat?
A: A hair chair

Q: What do you call a rodent's fedora or headgear?
A: A rat hat

Q: What would a feline use to play baseball
A: A cat bat

Q: What's another name for a portal that leads to the crawl space underneath a house?
A: A floor door

Q: What's another name for a ladle that could be used by astronauts after they land on this orb?
A: A moon spoon

Q: What do you call a relay competition between The Millenium Falcon, an X-Wing Fighters and Tie Fighters?
A: A space race

Q: What's the name of the road with butcher shops lined on both sides?
A: Meat street

Q: What's another name for a cherry-colored bunk?
A: A red bed

Q: What's another name for this black with white stripe stinky mammal's bed?
A: A skunk bunk

Q: What's another name for an amusing, harmless weapon?
A: A fun gun

Q: What do you call a magician's magical move using a red, rectangular block of sand and concrete materials?
A: A brick trick

Q: What do you call a speedy magician's magical move?
A: A quick trick

Q: What do you call the element or attribute that distinguishes Denzel Washington, Clint Eastwood, or Mel Gibson from the all the others?
A: Actor factor

Q: What do you call secret communication between bullfrogs?
A: Toad Code

Q: What do they call the street lined with bullfrogs?
A: Toad Road

Q: What do you call the mistake that a tall African animal makes?
A: A giraffe gaffe

Q: What do pirates ride in a parade?
A: A boat float

Q: What's a mailed note that's superior to the previous one?
A: A better letter

Q: What do you call measuring a cat for special outfits?
A: A kitten fittin'

Q: What do you call a round breakfast pastry made for a dog?
A: A beagle bagel

Q: What do you call when the king of the beasts doesn't tell the truth?
A: A lyin' lion

Q: What kind of shoes do owls wear in the winter?
A: A hoot boot

Q: What do you call a bird of prey that becomes a lawyer?

A: A legal eagle

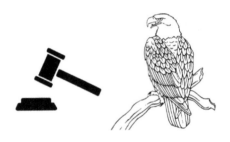

Q: What do guppies eat out of?

A: A fish dish

Q: What does another type of fish eat out of?

A: A sole bowl

Q: What do you call a rabbit with the sniffles?

A. A runny bunny.

Q: What do you call an argument between public transportation vehicles?

A: A bus fuss

Q: How does a male chicken get around town fast?

A: A rooster booster (like rocket boosters)

Q: Where do mediocre musicians play in the orchestra?
A: Middle fiddle

Q: What instrument did the infant play in the orchestra?
A: Little fiddle

Q: What's another name for a shy, bashful, young lad?
A: Coy boy

Q: What do you call an archer's weapon-for-shooting-arrows exhibition?
A: A bow show

Q: What's another name for fragile drinking-vessel-making lessons?
A: A glass class

Q: What's another name for the pastime in which movie celebrities aim to gain more popularity?
A: Fame game

Q: What do you call one of the seats that Goldilocks sat in?
A: Bear chair

Q: What's another name for head gear with the atlas of countries?
A: Map cap

# CHAPTER 13

# MORE Loads of Riddles, Jokes and Brain Teasers

Q: What goes Ha-ha-ha-bump?
A: Someone laughing their head off.

Q: What is green and smells like blue paint?
A: Green paint

Q: Why was the broom late?
A: Because it over-swept!

Q: What do workers do in a clock factory?
A: They make faces!

Q: When is a clock nervous?
A: When it's all wound up!

Q: What did the traffic light say to the car?
A: Look away please, I'm about to change!

Q: Why is Alabama the smartest state?
A: Because it has four A-s and one B!

Q: Which state has the smallest soft drinks?
A. Mini-Soda! (Minnesota)

Q: Where do oak trees come from?
A. OAKlahoma.

Q: How do you get an astronaut's baby to stop crying?
A: You rocket! (rock it)

Q: Did you hear about the claustrophobic astronaut?
A: He just needed a little space.

Q: Why did the bone chase the skull?
A: They wanted to get a-head

Q: Why did the teddy bear refuse dessert?
A: Because it was stuffed!

Q: What did one eye say to the other eye?
A: Something between us really smells.

Q: What did the sink say to the toilet?
A: Wow, you look really flushed!

Q: How many days are there in a year?
A: Only seven! Sunday, Monday, Tuesday,
Wednesday, Thursday, Friday and Saturday

Q: Why did the Cyclops principal close his school?
A: He had only one pupil!

Q: What is an owl's favorite type of math?
A: Owlgebra!

Q: Which restaurants are good at math?

A. Take-aways!

Q: Which performer is hired and fired by the circus on the same day?

A: The human canonball

Q: What is a reptile's favorite movie?

A: The Lizard of Oz

Q: What do you call a reptile that sings?

A. A RAPtile!

Q: What cookie does a bird like best?

A: Chocolate chirp

Q: Why did the bird get in trouble in class?

A: He was tweeting on a test. (play on words: cheating)

Q: What do you give a sick bird?
A: Tweetment!

Q: How did the bird break into the house?
A: With a crow bar!

Q: What kind of birds always stay together?
A. Velcrows. (play on words: Velcro)

Q: Where do pencils come from?
A: From Pencil-vania! (Pennsylvania)

Q: What did the paper say to the pencil?
A: Write on! (Right on!)

Q: Which hand is better to write with?
A: Neither. It's better to write with a pencil or a pen!

Q: Want to hear a joke about paper?
A: Never mind. It's tearable (terrible)

Q: How does a marathon racer say goodbye?
A: Gotta run

Q: How does a gardener say goodbye?
A: Seed you later!

Q: How does a bee say goodbye?
A: Gotta buzz

Q: How does a baseball player say goodbye?
A: Catch ya later!

Q: How does a salesman say goodbye?
A: Buy, buy! (Play on words: Bye bye!)

Q: How does a cheesemaker say goodbye?
A: Gouda bye!

Q: What does a vet keep outside his door?
A: A welcome mutt

Q: What kind of sports car do military attorneys drive?
A: JAG-uars

Q: What did the judge say when the skunk came into his courtroom?
A: "Odor in the court!"

Q: What is a porcupine's favorite game?
A. Poker.

Q: Why was George Washington buried on Mt. Vernon?
A: Because he was dead.

Q: What kind of bus crossed the ocean?
A. Christopher ColumBUS!

Q: What do you call two bananas?
A: A pair of slippers

Q: What do bananas do when they get a sunburn?
A. They peel.

Q: How do billboards talk?
A: Sign language.

Q: Why did busy musician spend so much time in bed?
A: Because he wrote sheet music.

Q: Why did the Grandma sit in the rocking chair with her roller blades on?
A. Because she wanted to rock and roll.

Q: Which planet is the best singer?
A: Nep-tune.

Q: What is a skeleton's favorite instrument?
A: A trom-bone

Q: What has many teeth but never bites?
A: A comb

Q: I'm a road that stretches from left to right. I'm often paved with pearly white. What am I?
A: A smile


Q: What did the baby lightbulb say to the Momma lightbulb?
A: I love you watts! (play on words: I love you lots!)


Q: What did one library book say to another library book?
A: Can I take you out?


Q: Why were there puddles on the beach?
A: Because of the seaweed


Q: Why did the scarecrow win a trophy?
A: Because he was outstanding in his field!


Q: What should a boxer drink before a fight?
A: Punch


Q: What did the inventor get when he crossed a turkey with an octopus?
A: Enough drumsticks for everyone at dinner.

Q: Which word is always pronounced wrong?
A: Wrong

Q: What time is the same, whether it goes backwards or forwards?
A: Noon (It's n-o-o-n whether spelled backwards or forwards)

Q: What word begins with "E" ends with "E" and sounds like it has only one letter in it?
A: Eye (sounds like the letter "I")

Q: What happens when a mouse marries a baker?
A: They have a cheesecake reception.

Q: Where do mice park their boats?
A: At the hickory dickory dock.

Q: What game do mice love to play?
A: Hide and squeak

Q: Why did the old house go to the doctor?
A: It was having window panes (play on words: pains)

Q: What kind of house is like a book?
A: A tall house. Because it has many stories.

Q: What's the sign of old age in a computer?
A: Loss of memory

Q: What's a computer's favorite thing to snack on at night?
A: Computer chips.

Q: How many books can you put in an empty backpack?
A: None. Because after that, then it won't be empty.

Q: What time is it when a princess is captured by a dragon?
A: Knight time!

Q: What is a parrot's favorite food on the 4th of July?
A. Fire crackers!

Q: Take me out of the box, scratch my head, I am now black but once was red. What am I?
A. A match!

Q: Why can only two elves sit under a toadstool?
A: There isn't mush-room (Play on words: much room)

Q: Which pillar is not used in a building?
A. A caterpillar.

Q: Why shouldn't you pollute the ocean?
A: Because you'll make the sea sick!

Q: What does a bee say when it comes down to the hive?
A: Hi honey, I'm home!

Q: What's the smartest type of insect?
A: A spelling bee.

Q: What do you call a tired gardener?
A: Bush-ed

Q: How did the gardener fix the broken tomato plants?
A: With tomato paste!

Q: What did one wall say to the other wall?
A: Meet me at the corner

Q: What years do frogs love the most?
A: Leap year

Q: What do you give a frog at a hospital?
A. A HOPeration!

Q: Why did the pigs win the football game against the sheep?

A: They had the home-snort advantage! (home court advantage)

Q: What do you get when you cross footwear with a mobile communication device?
A: Sock-so-phone (saxophone)

Q: What cheese doesn't belong to you?
A: Na-cho cheese (Not your cheese!)

Q: What's the correct way to put in a USB cord?
A: The other way.

Q: What is an irritating German car?
A: A Volkswagen Bug-gy

Q: What computer key is the astronauts' favorite?
A: The space bar

Q: Why did the sun go to school?
A: To become brighter.

Q: Why doesn't the sun need to go to college?
A. Because it has a million degrees!

Q: What do you call a family of Jewish comedians?
A: A Mishpochah-ha-ha (Mishpochah is the Jewish
word for "family")

Q: What store would you rarely find insects and flies
in?
A: A shoo store (shoe)

Q: Where do Chevrolets, Toyotas and other
automobiles like to go for fun?
A: A car-nival

Q: Where did the hunter go to look for a special
coat for his wife?
A: The fur-niture store

Q: What are hair stylists' favorite writing instruments?
A: Gel pens

Q: What are hair stylists' favorite amusement rides?
A: Roller coasters

Q: How do hair dressers get better at their jobs?
A: They brush up on their technique!

Q: Why did the photo go to prison?
A: Because it was framed!

Q: Why do bicycles fall over?
A: Because they're two-tired! (too tired)

Or

Q: Why couldn't the bike stand by itself?
A: It was two-tired.

Q: What's the difference between a poorly dressed man on a tricycle and a well-dressed man on a bicycle?
A: Attire

Q: How do you know when a bike is thinking?
A: You can see its wheels turning.

Q: Why is the word dark spelled with a K not a C?
A: Because you can't C in the dark.

Q: Why can't you ever tell a joke around glass?
A: It could crack up.

Q: How does Moses prepare his coffee?
A: Hebrews it.

Q: Why did the invisible man turn down the job offer?
A: Because he couldn't see himself doing it.

Q: Can February March?
A: No, but April May

Q: What did the pirate say at his 80th birthday party?
A: Aye Matey!

Q: What's a pirate's favorite subject in school?
A: Arrrrrrrrrrt.

Q: What's a pirate's other favorite subject in school?
A: Arrrrrrrrrrrithmetic.

Q: What's a pirate's favorite country to travel to?
A: Arrrgh-entina.

Q: Why did the professor wear his sunglasses to class?
A: Because his students were so bright.

Q: Why was the weightlifter upset?
A: She worked with dumbbells.

Q: Why did the boy put his money in the freezer?
A: He wanted cold, hard cash.

Q: Why don't scientists trust atoms?
A: Because they make up everything.

Q: Why did Mickey Mouse choose to become an astronaut?
A: He wanted to visit Pluto.

Q: What do you call a bunny with fleas?
A. Bugs Bunny.

Q: Why do we never tell jokes about pizza?
A: They're too cheesy.

Q: What type of music do balloons hate listening to?
A: Pop.

Q: Did you hear the joke about the roof?
A: Never mind, it's over your head.

Q: Where are average things manufactured?
A: The satis-factory.

Q: What did the first snowman say to and then ask the second snowman?
A: It smells like carrots over here! Do you smell carrots?

Q: What did the second snowman reply to the first snowman?
A: I don't smell carrots. But I do taste charcoal.

Q: What are bald sea captains most worried about?
A: Cap sizes.

Q: Why does Peter Pan fly around so much?
A: He Neverlands.

Q: Why mustn't you give Elsa a balloon?
A: She'll "Let It Go."

Fellowship of the Ring Joke

Q: What is the Grey Wizard's grandfather's name?

A: Grand-alf (Because the Grey Wizard's name is Gandalf)

Q: Why can't the music teacher start his car?

A: His keys are on the piano.

# The Lost Tractor Joke

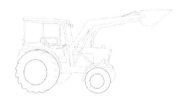

One day a farmer lost his tractor!

The news quickly spread among the farm animals.

One of the lambs asked his Dad: "Dad, how did the farmer lose his tractor?"

The Daddy sheep replied: "I don't know, son...*bleets* me!"

# CHAPTER 14

# Your Amazing BONUS!! SUMMER FUN Word Search

```
S V M O V I E S Q C V W I W V D S M
Z Q P V C A M P I N G A M R A T O U
L S K A T E B O A R D T P R C V W E
V X S C O O T E R O F E O B A A Q Z
P B P O P S I C L E S R O I T C E P
A Y E C I Y K I T E S S L C I A Z I
R P L A Y G R O U N D L R Y O T D C
T Z P I C E C R E A M I T C N I U N
I S I S W H L N P O O D D L R O D I
E U D W L H S W I M I E F E O N C C
S N I P Z Z B U F U N S O S I U U A
E R B L F R I S B E E S P G T G W B
```

Find the following words in the puzzle. Words are hidden → ↓ and ↘

| BEACH | BICYCLES | CAMPING | FRISBEES | FUN |
| ICE CREAM | KITES | MOVIES | PARTIES | PICNIC |
| PLAYGROUND | POOL | POPSICLES | SCOOTER | SKATEBOARD |
| SUN | SWIM | VACATION | WATERSLIDES | |

# ANSWERS TO YOUR
# AMAZING BONUS!!
# SUMMER FUN WORD SEARCH

```
                    Summer Fun

    .  .  M  O  V  I  E  S  .  .  .  W  .  .  V  .  .  .
    .  .  .  .  C  A  M  P  I  N  G  A  .  .  A  .  .  .
    .  S  K  A  T  E  B  O  A  R  D  T  P  .  C  V  .  .
    .  .  S  C  O  O  T  E  R  .  .  E  O  B  A  A  .  .
    P  B  P  O  P  S  I  C  L  E  S  R  O  I  T  C  .  P
    A  .  E  .  .  .  K  I  T  E  S  S  L  C  I  A  .  I
    R  P  L  A  Y  G  R  O  U  N  D  L  .  Y  O  T  .  C
    T  .  .  I  C  E  C  R  E  A  M  I  .  C  N  I  .  N
    I  S  .  .  .  H  .  .  .  .  D  .  L  .  O  .  I
    E  U  .  .  .  .  S  W  I  M  .  E  .  E  .  N  .  C
    S  N  .  .  .  .  .  .  F  U  N  S  .  S  .  .  .  .
    .  .  .  .  F  R  I  S  B  E  E  S  .  .  .  .  .  .
```

Word directions and start points are formatted: (Direction, X, Y)

BEACH (SE,9,4)
BICYCLES (SE,11,4)
CAMPING (SE,8,5)
FRISBEES (E,9,12)
FUN (E,15,3)
ICE CREAM (SE,10,2)
KITES (SE,11,2)

MOVIES (SE,13,3)
PARTIES (SE,7,3)
PICNIC (S,5,6)
PLAYGROUND (E,7,1)
POOL (SE,9,3)
POPSICLES (SE,4,3)
SCOOTER (S,4,5)

SKATEBOARD (S,3,2)
SUN (S,17,1)
SWIM (SE,13,7)
VACATION (S,1,1)
WATERSLIDES (SE,3,1)

Christmas Day 2020
Jim and Jackie, Michael and Alyssa

L→R: Alyssa, Jim, Jackie, and Michael – after they
successfully completed the 2021 Virginia Mason
Mother's Day 5K Walk/Run. Check out those medals!

# ABOUT THE AUTHORS

**James R. Morey** is a Software Engineer, Technology Consultant and a multiple-time #1 Bestselling Author. He is a top-rated Udemy Course Creator and a nationally recognized Book Writing and Publishing Coach.

Jim worked at Microsoft for over 18 years in server and Internet technologies including IIS, Operations Manager, SharePoint, and Azure, has written over

250K lines of code in C#, VB, javaScript, PowerShell, and has worked heavily in HTML5, CSS, T-SQL. Over the last seven years, he created several end-to-end marketing platforms.

Jim thoroughly enjoys traveling, bicycle riding, cooking, savoring delicious food from many different cultures, and is on a Keto-lifestyle. Most of all, he's a blessed Husband and a proud Dad of their two kids.

**Jackie Morey** is a multiple-time #1 International Bestselling Author, Book Publisher, Editor, Writing and Publishing Coach, Virtual Book Launch Host, Wife, and Mother of two children. When she's not homeschooling her kiddos, she enjoys traveling abroad with her Husband, especially to white sand, warm beaches with sky-colored water in the Philippines, playing chess with her children, having conversations over coffee with friends, watching movies with her family, reading, and enjoying food from many different countries.

She has coached hundreds of people from all walks of life – to help them write and publish their books –

business books, devotionals, non-fiction books, legacy books, Children's books and fiction books. She especially enjoys helping those who've dreamt of becoming authors for decades, to finally write the stories of their lives, and publish their unique message, their life lessons, and business books.

Jackie has launched dozens of select Premier Clients from zero idea to Bestselling Authors! She and her wonderful Husband Jim, have concocted their "secret sauce" and used this to help writers become authors, and authors become Bestselling Authors.

If you're interested in writing your business book, your Legacy book, a fiction book, a Children's book or any type of book series, connect with Jackie via email: CustomerStrategyAcademy@gmail.com and let her know what type of book you'd like to write.


**Michael Morey** is the eldest of two children to Jim and Jackie Morey. This is his second book. As of this publication, Michael is about to enter 6TH Grade. He enjoys playing with his Nerf guns, riding his scooter, swimming, building 3D model houses, solving Rubik's cubes, climbing trees, playing chess, bike riding, adult coloring books, adult dot-to-dot books, creating art projects, drawing sea creatures, solving puzzles, reading, building model cars, building Lego® Star Wars toy sets, and watching movies.

**Alyssa Morey** is the youngest of two children to Jim and Jackie Morey. This is her first book. As of this publication, Alyssa is about to enter 4TH Grade. She enjoys reading [she's a book worm], singing in choir, playing with her friends, writing stories [watch for her upcoming children's book novelettes and novellas], riding her scooter, dressing up in fancy party clothes, playing her ukulele, swimming, traveling, bike riding, making rubber band bracelets, writing letters to her pen pals, solving puzzles, and watching movies.

# YOUR FREE GIFT FOR CHECKING OUT OUR BOOK

🎁 Thank you for checking out our book! Our family would like to give **you** a FREE gift!!

Jim and Jackie's business friend – Jay Boyer – who's a Children's Book Bestselling Author and who makes thousands of dollars every month from his children's books, did a <u>value-packed</u> webinar called "**How to Write and Publish a #1 Bestselling Children's Book.**"

Click here now to watch it ➜
<u>https://bit.ly/ChildrensBookJackieMorey1</u>

👍 If you've always wanted to write a Children's Book, **this** is the webinar to watch. You'll even discover one of the *best niches* to write children's books for! Click the link below to access your FREE gift now...

🎁 → https://bit.ly/ChildrensBookJackieMorey1

# PLEASE RATE OUR BOOK

My Family and I would be honored if you would please take a few moments to rate our book on Amazon.com (U.S.).

<u>Or, if you're in any of these countries, please use these Amazon sites:</u>

Amazon.ca (Canada)

Amazon.co.uk (U.K.)

Amazon.com.au (Australia)

Amazon.fr (France)

Amazon.de (Germany)

Amazon.co.jp (Japan)

Amazon.com.mx (Mexico)

Amazon.es (Spain)

A 5-star rating and a short review (e.g. "Jam-packed with FUN riddles and jokes!" or "Thoroughly enjoyed it!") would be much appreciated. We welcome longer, positive comments as well.

If you feel like this book should be rated at three stars or fewer, please hold off posting your comments on Amazon. Instead, please send your feedback directly to me (Jackie), so that we can use it to improve the next edition. We're committed to providing the best value to our customers and readers, and your thoughts can make that possible.

You can reach me at <u>CustomerStrategyAcademy@gmail.com</u>.

Thank you very much!

To your success and prosperity with a purpose,

*Jackie Morey*
Publisher-Collaborative Author
Multiple #1 International Bestselling Author

Lightning Source UK Ltd.
Milton Keynes UK
UKHW020158031221
394997UK00009B/2707

9 781733 250184